I0164192

Downish.

Tears Apart

by

Ideas with Ink

Copyright © 2018 Ideas with Ink
All rights reserved.
101 Panya Publishing
101panya@gmail.com
ISBN-13: 978-1988880075
ISBN-10: 1988880076
BISAC: POE011000

Table of Contents

I wanted to kill myself by doing nothing, but I did everything.

Life is a Metronome

Life is a metronome.
Somebody dies and someone is born.
Somebody does something every second.
Somebody goes to bed,
And somebody else wakes up.

Life is a metronome.
A guy drinks a glass of water with four cubes of ice in it.
A boy makes a chocolate cake with pink icing.
A guy wears a pink shirt to school and he is not afraid.
A man directs a short film where a zebra and a lion eloped to the moon.
A girl discovers a new star and names it after her dog.
A schoolgirl wins the spelling bee with the word "hopeful".
A woman writes a poem about two countries eating a border for dinner.

Life is a metronome.
A queer kid just gets put out onto the street because her parents didn't accept her.
A girl's privates are mutilated because she was born a girl.
A woman has to pay for a tampon.
A guy discovers he has cancer.
A woman discovers her cancer diagnosis was wrong.
A minority didn't get the promotion.
A guy writes lies on his resume about finding the cure for AIDS.

A girl finds out she got rejected from her dream school.
A guy tries alcohol for the first and last time.
A gay man gets sent to jail for loving another guy.
A kid dyes his hair sky blue.
Another kid gets his ears pierced.
A girl orders the wrong textbook online.

Life is a metronome.
Some school opens up for rural kids.
A house gets foreclosed because a man left his family.
A vegan cafe opens up.
Thousands of animals are slaughtered for burgers.
A thousand trees get chopped down.
A Japanese garden opens up.
A river gets polluted.
A lake gets cleaned.
A town legalizes pot.
A coal mine shuts down.
A bus crashes into another bus.
A rocket ship lands on Mars.

Life is a metronome.
Somebody says, "I love you",
And somebody responds, "I love you, too",
And someone walks by his crush knowing he wasn't gay,
And some guy on Tinder swipes left a minority girl.
Two people fall in love,
And two people break up.
Two people become three people.

Life is a metronome.
A book just starts to be written with the words "He loved her".
And a baby takes her first steps.
Some kid fails a math test.
And across the world another kid aces his math test.
A dad packs a PB & J without crusts for his son.
A woman visits a psychologist and talks about clouds.
And a son visits his dad in the hospital.
A girl votes for the first time,
And another girl is proud she is Muslim.

Life is a metronome.
Somebody kills herself because she was bullied.
Some girl is slut-shamed, even though she is beautiful.
Some guy is fat-shamed, even though he is beautiful.
Somebody comes out to his immigrant parents.
Some girl takes her girlfriend to the prom, and they are happy.
A woman sees her child for the first time.
A man sees his child for the last time.

Life is a metronome.
Some stupid video about a cat falling in love with a dog goes viral.
Some movie about two people driving from LA to NYC comes out,
And another movie - about a white man buying a mansion in Upstate New York.

A song comes out about a victim becoming a survivor,
And another song about a Sky and an Ocean having a kid named Earth.

Life is a metronome.
A police officer shoots a black man,
And a black man gets shot by a police officer.
A woman throws out her letter for jury duty,
And a jury sentences a black man to life for a crime he didn't commit,
And acquits a white man who committed the crime.
A mentally ill man is executed.
A woman is acquitted of raping a man.

Life is a metronome.
Somebody wins the lottery.
Somebody buys $100 worth of lottery tickets and wins nothing.
Somebody buys a pair of jeans,
And somebody else buys a loaf of bread,
Or a pack of cigars,
Or a puppy,
Or a pregnancy test.

Life is a metronome.
A Latina gets her Green Card.
An Asian guy gets his Canadian Citizenship.
An Asian guy and a Latina fall in love.
An Asian guy and a Latina have a kid.
A kid goes to school.
A kid writes a poem.
A kid publishes a poem.

Life is a metronome,
And every human is a single note
In the song that is called

Love.

I wanted to kill myself by hanging with the wrong crowd, but I left the social circle.

Hope

The house with no windows.
The tree that has no leaves.
The river with no fish.
The road with no people.

The music with no notes.
The story without words.
The dinner with no bread.
The rose without thorns.

That is how life with
                    no hope.

Betrayal

When friends turn foe
You feel as if you are alone.
Life is a never-ending show:

Smile, learn, cry, laugh and grow!
Plough
Through days and years
To conquer all your darkest fears.

Farewell

Farewell, my friend, farewell.
Farewell till the end, farewell.
Train will take you or plane
On its wings to the sky, -
Time to fly, time to fly.

> Time has come to depart,
> Time has come to depart,
> Be apart from each other.
> No tears or longing to stay.
> Take good wishes and pray.

Pray for love and for friendship.
Pray for love and for friendship.
Don't forget but forgive
All the pain and despair.
And your soul might be spared…

Forgiveness

Forgive me for all the sins,
For past, for present and future,
For the road that never ends,
For the blood that I've shed,
For the hopes that I've lost,
For the pain that I've caused.

Don't be jealous of me:
My pocket is full of money.
My heart is full of hate,
There is no heaven's gate.
My hands are full of blood,
My eyes are full of loss.
There is **no end to wars**.

Unborn

What if I never was born?
My heart was never torn.
No birthday cake with candles.
No zits or my love handles.

No first love or break ups.
No hot chocolate in mugs.
No licks of my happy dog.
No city covered in fog.

No sunsets or sunrises.
No births or fast demises.
No starchy shirts and pants.
No cities through my lens.

No more tears or winnings.
No more ends or beginnings.
What if I never was born?
Then I wouldn't miss this world.

I wanted to kill myself by falling out of love, but gravity doesn't exist in my heart.

You're a Hero

Who touched your heart?
The one, who broke it.
Who slapped your cheek?
The one, who kissed it.

Who covered her with insults?
Same, who showered with hugs.
Who abandoned his child?
Same, who gave her life.

Who restored your dignity?
The one, who never left.
Who lifted up your spirit?
The one, whose name is **you**.

The End

A lonely day.
A lonely night.
Half eaten bread.
A silent goodbye.

Unspoken words.
Unfinished tea.
This is the end.
Of you and me.

Will Not

Four arms intertwined.
The trains are about to leave.
Time stopped in silence,
Scared to tell them the truth.

They whisper goodbyes,
Which will become farewell.
The sound of their trains' bells
Will turn into canon's deep hell.

The border will cut their flesh.
The war will possess what they had,
As if it was a righteous payback
For those arms intertwined.

Why?

Why do we die?
Why do we live?
With a light
and a night,
With a tear
and a smile,
With a heart ,
that is ready
                to give...

Might

In an open window I see leaves, I see sky,
Sun and clouds, roads from planes.
Where do they take you, these roads?
To a new country, a city, or a town,
Where life is as bright as a party clown?

You eat dinner at a diner with a broken light.
In an open window you see parked cars
Where do drivers go? Alone, home
To watch TV and read papers?
To eat dinner from plastic containers?
To dream about new day in the darkness of
night?

Look out of the window and see the leaves,
See the sky and the planes, the diner,
Parked cars, people who walk the dark streets.
There is a hope that the day will bring light.

It just might.
                It just might.

Full of I

Come and sing with me,
      For all these years
I forgot the lullabies.
      Come and sit with me,
For all these years
      There are no ties.

The joy full of joy.
      The death full of death.
The love full of love.
      The truth full of truth.
The pain full of pain.
      The rain full of rain.
            The eye full of *I.*

Fall

Through darkness,
    Through pain and despair,
        Through cries and betrayal
            I walked to you.

                I followed the voice,
        That was inside,
    That guided me.
I walked to you.

Then
I stumbled
And
            Fell.

I wanted to kill myself by fighting in a war against myself, but I signed a peace-treaty.

To End or Not to End

Raw as if my soul is a piece of meat
Butchered and left on a table to bleed.
Raw as if tortured inside my head.
Hang to my life by invisible thread.

Disoriented and lost within circle of time,
As if in a circus arena covered in slime.
Inverted and sucked into a black hole.
Stopped all attempts to be a happy whole.

My silent screams only heard in my head,
Tell me to end it and not suffer like that.
A light in my soul shows the uncut thread,
I put scissors down and hold it instead.

Loner

I sit in my room, alone,
Not forgotten, but unknown
To the world outside my space,
As if I exist without a trace.

I write in my room, alone,
Fill pages with lands and homes,
People and rare creatures
No taller, than couple of inches.

I dream in my room, alone
About places I want to go.
I talk to people in my head
Whom I never even met.

I think in my room, alone,
Out of my comfort zone.
I open the door and leave,
Finally ready to go and **live**.

The Doubt

Are you scared of what will happen?
Are you afraid of what will not?
Of the roads not planned or taken?
Of the people you met, but forgot?

    Are you happy of what will happen?
    Are you sad of what will not?
    Of the people whom you will face?
    Of the battles you fought, but lost?

Are you proud of what will happen?
Are you angry of what will not?
Of the dreams that never made it?
Of the hopes that were bluntly shot?

    Don't be scared, happy, or saddened
    By the chain of your future or past.
    Live to the fullest and don't extinguish
    The fire inside you too fast.

Lives Lived

In my past life I was a star,
Cold, lonely, sparkly, distant.
I watched the Earth from afar.
Didn't love anyone or missed.

In my past life I was a horse,
Fought many battles and wars,
Was slaughtered without remorse.

In my present life I am me.
I try to be peaceful and free.

To Belong

I stay at the edge of my time
Covered in minutes as flies,
As a victim of a violent crime.

I stay at the edge of my mind
Covered in thoughts as lies,
As a pickle in a tangy brine.

I stay at the edge of the world
In a humble attempt to belong.

So be It

So be it. Life.
Everyday strife.

So be it. Loss,
Sickness and a cross.

So be it. Love.
Fits like a glove.

So be it. Death.
A coffin and a wreath.

So be it. Me.
Glasses and braces.
Embrace it!

I wanted to commit suicide by losing the game of life, but the world was cheating.

Senses

I can **see**,
But I'm **blind**ed by
Fake people.

I can **hear**,
But wars
Make me **deaf**.

I can feel,
But pain
Numbs everything.

I have all **sense**s,
But life doesn't
Make any **sense**.

What?

What are tears,
If not a liquid
Of a soul's blood?

What is laughter,
If not a music
Of a soul's orchestra?

What is breath,
If not a sign
Of a soul's life?

Trying

Knock on a door,
Once, twice,
Knock until
Knuckles bleed.

Climb a ladder,
High, higher,
Climb until
Feet seize.

Bang on a window
Loud, louder,
Bang until
It shatters.

Splattered blood.
Pieces of glass.
Broken past.

Non-Existence

In a hole, abandoned,
Trashed into shreds,
As if an old rug
Ripped into threads.

In a hole, curled up,
As an aborted flesh,
Never loved or hugged,
Turned into thresh.

In a hole, lifeless,
As a numbered corpse,
Longed for love,
Left with remorse.

Two Sides

If I was loved by you,
How would that feel?
Warm as wool socks?
Sweet as an apple pie?
Happy as a birthday?

       Completed.

If I wasn't loved by you,
How would that feel?
Cold as a bucket of ice?
Sour as lemon juice?
Sad as a departure?

       Deleted.

My Companions

I bought the glasses for the moon
To read me stories when it's **dark**.

I bought the umbrella for the road
To walk alongside me when it's **rainy**.

I bought the drum set for the sun
To play with me when I am **happy**.

Life or death

How could I tell
If it is simply life,
Or life's deadly spell?

Broken voices,
Abandoned dreams,
Corrupted choices?

How could I feel
If it is simply death
Or death's soul mill?

The End

When it ends
Does it simply die,
Or bleeds first,
Then rots
While you
Feel *deprived*?

When it ends
Does it leave you
Empty from loss,
Filled with
Remorse
Or *revived*?

*I wanted to kill myself by becoming nobody, but
I became somebody.*

I am. I was

I am young.
I stare at clouds.
I eat ice cream.
I read books.
I write naive poems.
I kiss and hug.
I laugh and cry.
I die
In a war
I died.
I laughed and cried
I kissed and hugged.
I wrote naive poems.
I read books.
I ate ice cream.
I stared at clouds.
I was young.

Fleshy Ghost

A shadow without an object.
A raven with a broken wing.
A song without any notes.
A necklace without a string.

> I walk through life and halls,
> No friends, anyone to bond.
> Out of place, invisible, lost,
> In between worlds as a ghost.

A shadow, that reflects stars.
A raven, that walks over cliffs.
A song, that exists as a score.
Pearls still left in shells in reefs.

Who Would I be?

If I wasn't me?
Who would I be?

A killer bee?
A rooted tree?
A shiny star?
A Russian tsar?
A travelled road?
A prince toad?

Whatever I ponder
Cannot change
Current yonder.

The Creation of You

I will draw your portrait.

Blue from the river for eyes.
Auburn from oak leaves for hair,
Wind will style the strands.
Sunset will colour your cheeks.

Ocean pearls for your smile.
Stars will light up your heart.
Tree brunches will be your body.
Thunder will become your voice.

Night will make you **mortal**.

After

A lifeline as clear as a river
Connected to a tiny vein.
The world outside is white.
I shiver.
She cries,
She knows that *I will die*.

But why?

She would rather die.
She fights
Her tears.
She smiles.
The world inside is bright,
Filled with our memories,
Her lifeline when I demise.

Whispers

The night whispers secrets
To butterflies in a distance.

The day whispers stories
To brown bears in a forest.

The time whispers dreams
To souls stuck in a realm.

Stop!

Stop!
I was told many times.
Don't run, but walk.
Don't be quiet,
Talk!
Don't sit around,
Get up!
Don't cry and be sad,
Live and laugh!

> Stop!
> I tell the world today
> What I feel and say.
> If I want to run,
> I charge!
> If I want to think,
> Sit, cry or laugh,
> I don't ask a permission,
> I simply act.

Bullying Kills

Why do you think that
It does not hurt
When you call me fat,
Ugly, useless brat?

Why do you think that
You have the right
To tear my heart,
To break my plight?

Why do you think that
When I am gone
It was just a joke,
But not *your* fault?

A Little Boy

A little boy as I once was:
Short brown hair,
Glasses on freckled nose.

Played with shiny rocks,
Built paper boats,
Sailed them farther,
Squabbled with his brother,

Slept in on Sundays,
Walked his dog,
Drew castles and people,
Was afraid of frogs,

Scribbled words on paper,
Snuggled with his mother,
Put so many things for later,
Worked with his father.

A little boy as I once was
Perished many sleeps ago
In Holocaust.

Broken Whole

I am the ocean of
Drowned dreams.
It seems
As if time froze
In an instance
When you and me
Created distance
From promises,
White lies,
Half-truths,
As if we thought
We were immortal,
When we were
Never whole,

But broken.

Self-Doubt

A black hole
Swallows me.
I try to be whole,
But I break
Into pieces
And disintegrate.
Feel useless,
Abused by me.

Why is it this way
When I want to be
Not happy, but free
From those thoughts
And habits?
But life goes on
While I am still
In a hole.

A Revival

I walked the streets in my mind,
The ones, that I liked as a child:
Green trees and cobble stones.
You were dead, I was **alone**.

I walked the streets in my dream,
The ones, that I liked as a teen:
No trees, just rails and trains.
You were dead, I was **in chains**.

I walked the streets step by step,
The ones, that have no end:
Open road filled with vibe.
You were dead, I was **alive**.

I Will

If you had one wish
What would it be?

To build or demolish
Lies,
Lives?

Open or shut
Doors,
Eyes?

Take or give
Words,
Dreams?

If I had a wish to fulfill
I will.

I wanted to kill myself by becoming a chameleon, but I lived in a black and white world.

My Dream

My
dream
is
to
live
in
a world
where
people
are
people.

A Carbon Copy

I wake up,
Get ready,
Go to school,
Sit in classes,
Eat lunch,
Go home,
Do projects,
Fall asleep.

> Everyday is
> A *carbon* copy
> Of yesterday.

I plan my escape.
I run red lights,
I swim oceans,
I kiss mermaids,
I sing with stars,
I build castles.
I wake up.

Cutters

Flesh.
Fresh.
I am not good enough
For them,
For you,
For me.

Flesh
Unleashed,
As if I can carve
New me
For you,
For them.

In an attempt
To be
Just me
I cut all ties,
                 Not me.

We Are

I have few things.
You have none.
How does it matter?
My pain is not bigger.
Yours is not better.

My struggle is real.
Your strife is right.
The human nature
Is what can unite
You, me, them, us.

Dead

You are dead.
I question why?
Where did you go?
Do you feel
What I feel,
That I am alone,
As if my chest was open,
The heart replaced
By a weighted rock.

You were my rock,
My everything,
My silence, and my song.
Now, when you're gone,
Everyone tells me
To remain strong,
But all I want
Is to cry on your shoulder,
Which isn't here any longer.

So I carry you along
As my weightless rock.

Music

Listen to the music of the forest.
Mermaids whisper,
Birds whistle.

Listen to the music of the city.
Rails drum,
People roam.

Listen to the music of the soul.
Always on,
Always strong.

Faith or Fate?

Is it fate or faith
That brought
Us together?

Smoggy air.
Slippery steps.
Skipped breaths.
Brittle moment.
Barred kiss.
Bolted embrace.

Not faith or fate
Brought us together,
But both drew us

Apart.

Depressed

Floored and gloomy.
Lost for words.
Destroyed
By the past,
Which is
No longer to last.

Faulted and desperate,
Lost for thoughts.
Betrayed
By the actions,
That are
Now destruction.

Hurt and miserable,
Lost for tears.
Abandoned
By the one,
Who is
No longer the one.

The Space

Fallen leaves as bitter tears
Covered the face of the Earth.
Frozen rivers dressed her in lace.
Trees have provided rooted place.

Still, she is not at peace with herself,
Needs to find purpose and space
To grow, to bleed, to cry, to exist
In a universe that is hard **to resist**.

I wanted to kill myself by scuba diving in the river of death, but I stayed on the sands of time.

I will Stand Behind You

I will stand behind you
No matter what.
If it rains or snows.
During peace or war.

I will stand behind you
No matter why.
If you sad or happy.
During death or life.

I will stand behind you
No matter what.
No matter why.

If We Were Stories

Once many moons ago
There was a girl
With a heart
Fresh as a snow,
Cold as a snow,
Soft as a snow,
That never loved,
That was never loved.

She met someone
With a heart
Black as a coal,
Cold as a coal,
Hard as a coal,
Who loved,
Who was burnt.

So they joined
As one
The circle of life.

You and Me

Here is you.
Here is me.
Polarity unites
When we say
The opposite things.

There is you.
There is me.
Polarity divides
When we feel
The similar things.

You and me apart.
An empty space
Between us,
A weightless mind,
An *existence*.

An Outcast

The boy who plays alone,
Who talks to himself,
An invisible person,
With invisible friends.

Looked down upon,
Looked through,
As if his life's canvas
Is a clear window.

He is an outcast
By the crowd outside.
He wants *to belong*
As you and I.

A Friend's Suicide

An empty spot,
A chair
You used to sit.
Not anymore.

Why did you do it?
Was it an impulse?
Was it a joke?
Or a cry for help?

I won't know ever.
I will remember.
The way you **were**.

The Hold

I will hold your hand
In mine
Until you want me to,
Until you pull away,
Until I pull through.

        You will hold my hand
        In yours
        Until I hold you,
        Until you let go,
        Until you disappear.

I wanted to kill myself by diving into another dimension, but I swam in the sea of people.

Media Kills

A live picture on the wall
Fills my heart with fear,
So far, but so near
Someone's pain and joy,
Broken trees, burnt cities,
Abandoned children,
Injured soldiers,
Fake problems,
Overblown emotions.

I can control this reality.
The real world is out of
Reach.
How do we change
The stories that we preach?

Start with
One word,
One human.
Change **you**.

Reality

What is a reality,
If not an imprint
Of people and things,
Dreams and ghosts?

You can tune in,
You can tune out.
You can erase or create.

What if the reality
We live and know
Is just a movie,
That plays in your head
Until you are *dead*?

Nothing Lasts

Dwindled on time:
The fleeted past
Seeped through
My frozen fingers,
Vanished into dust.

I held onto memories:
Now just photographs,
Filled with pain,
Covered in tears,
Sprinkled with laughs.

Nothing lasts.

Love Is

I fell in love with you,
Fell deeply nowhere.
A fall from grace.
I lost my face.
I crushed the pace.
Loved and didn't care.

Give me the strength.
Give me the wisdom.
Give me the art to let go.
Through the distance,
Through the snow,
Let me forget the sorrow.

I leave behind this pain.
I leave behind this love.
I shut the heart.
I break the life,
I turn the light behind
To live the soul's night.

To Let Go

Forced to let go or
Blessed that it left?
Do I feel like a thief,
Or a victim of theft?

Why do I bleed
From the inside out?
Why do I speak from
Quiet to loud?

Was it a human,
A thought, or a thing?
I didn't have a choice,
It **was taken** from me.

Dead Us

Street lamps,
Tram rails,
Dusted oaks,
Lonely cats.

Steeped tea.
Frozen glass.
Broken heart.
Dead us.

I wanted to kill myself by getting stuck in one of society's traps, but I didn't fit inside the box.

Opposites Attract

I say, "Yes." You say, "No."
I say, "Stop." You say, "Go."
I say "Day." You say, "Night."
I say "Dark." You say "Light."

I say, "Rain." You say, "Snow."
I say, "Keep." You say, "Throw."
I say, "Dull." You say, "Sharp."
I say, "Flute." You say, "Harp."

    Opposites attract
    Like white and black.
    Opposite unite
    In death and life.

I say, "South." You say, "North."
I say, "Sky." You say, "Earth."
I say, "Free." You say, "Chain."
I say, "Love." You say, "Pain."

There is magic in your eyes.
There are sea and sky.
There is twinkle in your smile
Makes me want to fly.

    Opposites attract
    Like white and black.
    Opposite unite
    In death and life.

Fly away with me,
Don't think; don't say!

Let your heart be free
And stay that way!

Opposites attract
Like white and black.
Opposite unite
In death and life.

Not Giving Up

Climb a mountain,
Fall and get up.

> My knees are scraped.
> My palms are dirty.
> My soul is wounded.
> My spirit is strong.

> > If I don't know what
> > Fall is,
> > How can I appreciate
> > The sunset and the sunrise
> > Atop the mountain?

Saying Goodbye

I say goodbye with my heart and eyes.
I say goodbye without tears and cries.
I leave behind a part of my soul.
I keep all the memories in a vault.

Saying goodbye
I wonder – why?
Why should I die
Saying goodbye?

Promise of love and future together
Turned into dust for ever and ever.
Nothing to say, frozen and still,
I wanted to stay, but will leave at will.

Saying goodbye:
I know – why.
Don't have to lie
Saying goodbye.

Never turned back to be with you.
Divided by destiny one love into two.
Broken heart stitched back by choice
Always to have my own will and voice.

Saying goodbye
Between you and I.
Sever the tie by
Saying goodbye.

Saying goodbye.
Saying goodbye…

Grateful

Grateful for highs
And grateful for lows.

Grateful for sunny days
And for the first snow.

Grateful for enemies
And for the friends.

Grateful for the beginnings
And for the inevitable end.

Why Do I Write?

I write not because I can,
But rather because I cannot
Leave the words inside me,
The ones, that need to be told.

I write because I can say
Things that I know and don't,
Not because I have to,
But simply because I want.

I wanted to kill myself by polluting my own world, but I planted my own family tree.

About the Author

Ideas with Ink is a pen name of a young Canadian Author who was born and raised in Toronto, Canada.

He connects with his readers through intriguing poetry and prose, mind-boggling play on words quotes, art and videos.

His writing can be summoned in his quote, "I tried to kill myself by suffocating in the reality, but I found a door that led to a parallel universe."

He has published his first poetry collection "Time Capsule" and his second poetic existential novel "nothing" about life and death in 2017. His provocative novel "100 People who Changed my World" was released in the Spring of 2018

He is a vegetarian and has written a children's story "Why am I Vegetarian?" under Mama Bear name. More books in The Tiger Family stories are coming soon:

- Story Two "Why Don't I look Like My Parents?"
- Story Three "Why Do the Words Hurt?"

His poem for children "The Dragon in the Glass Ball" is about loss, love and hope.

All available in paperback and e-book on Amazon and www.101panyapublishing.com

Please follow him on FB, IG, and Twitter @ideaswithink.

You can contact the author by e-mail at ideaswithink@gmail.com.

All rights reserved 2018 ©
www.ideaswithink.com
101 Panya Publishing
101panya@gmail.com

No part of this book may be reproduced or transmitted in any form or by any means, electronic or mechanical, including photocopying, recording or by any information storage and retrieval system, without written permission from the author.

To protect the privacy of certain individuals the names and identifying details have been changed.

This is a work of fiction. Any names or characters, businesses or places, events or incidents, are fictitious. Any resemblance to actual persons, living or dead, or actual events is purely coincidental.

www.ingramcontent.com/pod-product-compliance
Lightning Source LLC
Chambersburg PA
CBHW060529030426
42337CB00021B/4188